HOUSE OF MYTH AND NECESSITY

HOUSE OF

JENNIFER

A SUTHER

Praise for HOUSE OF MYTH AND NECESSITY

"Jennifer Sutherland once told me that, as a poet, she sometimes feels as if she's trying to fit a square peg into a round hole. I beg to differ. In her *House of Myth and Necessity*, Sutherland creates a geometry entirely of her own. In this witty, wide-ranging collection, the wisdoms of her fields (language, law, lore [Greek myth and Baltimore]) blend seamlessly and synergistically into an entirely new shape. This House creates and then fills a completely new (and necessary) space in contemporary poetry."

—MOIRA EGAN, author of *The Furies*

"The poems in Jennifer A. Sutherland's *House of Myth and Necessity* are wildly inventive—modeled after the Fibonacci sequence, a legal cross examination, and a panopticon, to name a few of her forms—and also deeply moving. Alcestis (a lesser known but fascinating character from a Euripides play) shows up repeatedly, but rarely in the same scaffolding: she is a saltine, the hanger from *Mommie Dearest*, and often herself (and so many of us): a woman struggling to find her voice after all she has already seen. These poems are brave and complex, and yet this book is also *fun*; I guarantee you will want to read it again and again."

—LYNN MELNICK, author of *I've Had to Think Up a Way to Survive*

"The poems in Jennifer A Sutherland's *House of Myth and Necessity* dare to enter the rooms of memory and trauma, to speak a story 'when it's returned from dead.' With Alcestis as her muse, Sutherland admits us 'through a side door' to bear witness to a story about domestic violence and how 'we don't always know disaster as disaster when it arrives'—a story that all too often goes unspoken. These poems interrogate and deconstruct cultural myths about female sexuality and womanhood, about being a wife and mother, about the real cost of difficult choices: 'There's good or there's pragmatic, a terrible dilemma.' Sutherland's poems know this hard truth, just as they know how easily an "opened bone becomes a window." But they also speak to the beauty of survival, which is everywhere evident in Sutherland's lyrical precision and skillful use of language. This is a brave, powerful, and necessary collection."

—AMANDA NEWELL, author of *Postmortem Say*

"'No woman is as innocent or as austere as the writer makes her'—in *House of Myth and Necessity*, Jennifer A Sutherland explores this idea through her deep knowledge of the law and the myth of Alcestis. The speaker's experience of regret and loss, violence and agency, is viewed through the lens of the Euripides myth, using the language of film, mathematics, and law to question the choices we make and the intentions we have in making them. All lives are made of myth and necessity, and what we need is often brought to us through stories; this particular story of choices, consequences, and questions reminds us, 'Sometimes you have to read between the lines, coin a phrase . . .' to make new meaning. This collection is challenging, intelligent, and unlike anything I've read lately. Brava."

—DONNA VORREYER, author of *Unrivered*

MYTH AND NECESSITY

AND

RIVER RIVER BOOKS
Durham, North Carolina

Published in the United States of America

Library of Congress Cataloging-in-Publication Data
Sutherland, Jennifer A, 1972–
House of Myth and Necessity / Jennifer A Sutherland.
ISBN-13: 979-8-9926116-3-2
Subjects: LCSH: American Poetry, Women's Poetry, Law, Myth, Mathematics.
LCGFT: Poetry.
LCCN: 2025941903

Cover and interior design by Alban Fischer
Cover art: Jean-François Pierre Peyron, *Alceste mourante*, 1985. Public domain.

RIVER RIVER BOOKS
10 Linganore Place
Durham, NC 27707

www.riverriverbooks.org

Contents

As if to say, within every death a life stands waiting to be set free, should anyone have the nerve to do it. As if to say, try looking deep into a house, a marriage, or an idea like Necessity and you will see clear through it to the other side.

—ANNE CARSON

Preface to Euripedes' *Alcestis*

Alcestis as Res Ipsa

Loquitur. One day I opened up
the kitchen window and ushered in
a butterfly. You will recognize the metaphor,
and what it meant: that I loved someone
else. I know it wasn't what you wanted to hear.

But count up all the years
you undertook to chamber me. More
than six, the perfect number. Your own peculiar
passage vanquished you, you yielded
all the way to ash and spit

your venom out at breakfast. By night you
were a rimy ferryman, obol-eyed and wary.
I don't know what I'm saying.

I'm saying, sorry.

Alcestis as a Trial, an Ekstasis, a Whereas, or a Problem

After Anne Carson

WHEREAS, an advocate begins by defining terms;

WHEREAS, an advocate undertaking argument speaks carefully;

WHEREAS, neither of these propositions is completely accurate; in both cases, an advocate begins by choosing sides. The right speech, the person who is *in the right*, the situation fortune favors;

WHEREAS, this is not a simple proposition; everyone is sure *no jury in the world* etc. etc.;

WHEREAS, everyone asks the judge or jury for objective reassurance of their innocences, and the judge or jury might or might not answer in the anticipated way;

WHEREAS, the preceding sentence is beautiful; it is a gorgeous thing, pivoting as it does upon its variables, its *ors;*

WHEREAS, the word *ors* functions as the opposite of its homonym, since it arrests the movement of the rhetoric and leaves the idea stranded in the water, the waves lapping gently at the bow, waiting for the mist to clear;

WHEREAS, the sentence remains where it is as surely as if it was anchored to the ocean floor;

WHEREAS, for poems contemplating and assessing fault in several parties, there are any number of analogies to be found in literature or myth;

WHEREAS, *Oresteia* is an obvious choice, with its curses, murders, and its vengeful Furies. People kill and then are killed in retribution, one after the other, until finally Orestes pleads insanity and lives;

WHEREAS, the eponymous heroine of *Antigone* privileges one system's laws over another's and then she dies, and even if she only hangs herself a whole family hangs with her. And anyway the lady dies;

WHEREAS, Alcestis, the lady and the play, is intensely in-between, innocent or guilty, alive or dead;

WHEREAS, she will not bear direct examination. She covers her face and keeps to her secluded places;

WHEREAS, if you wish to visit with her she'll admit you but only through a side door, after you have traversed a trail that leads through a wood, your shoes soaked through with river water;

WHEREAS, in the middle of *Alcestis* lies a woman and her grieving children, even though the people watching from the bleachers expect a satyr, nymphs, a monster, and a wineskin;

WHEREAS, Heracles arrives, a *machina*, not a *deus*, and he returns the mother to her children;

WHEREAS, Alcestis holds her tongue;

WHEREAS, the gods have very little to do with any of it; and,

Looking deeply into the house, the rooms converge on one another, caress one another, birth and suckle and then destroy one another, which is Necessity. Necessity leaps upon the concave back of the gazelle, who yelps in terror, struggles and then succumbs.

Necessity eats until it is full. The air moves the grass like a curtain drawn open and then closed.

Alcestis as a Hon, but Not the Kitschy, Cute Kind

There were like 3 clubs worth going to
and we went to none of them.

Our accents were mostly different and a little
the same. Your York Rd. U and my Blair Rd.—

you have to be from here to understand.
It's Belair. I have to explain what people

can't figure out for themselves but they hate it
when I do. I rode the No. 15 down to Erdman Ave.

My little brother got sepsis
playing out back behind the house, in the alley,

he dunked his foot into a hole filled up with rain
and rat shit. Meanwhile, husband, you were living just down

the street from a pool club and Jim Palmer. He used
to crash his poppy-red Corvette right through the middle

of the ball game like a line drive, like
he didn't give a crap about the batter or the basemen

because he didn't. No one liked him either, not even
the Artie Donovan-era farts who sat around

the Valley Inn popping Natty Bohs, which were shit
beers then too. This is not me being wistful for the neighborhood,

just me putting two and two together while I write this down,
how you always knew when I'd been to your apartment

while you weren't there from tiny clues I guess I left
behind. Maybe the carpet looked less impeccably new

because I shed some skin cells on it or I moved a coaster
on the coffee table one quarter millimeter to the right.

You were such a stickler for things being exactly how
you wanted them. When you were twelve you soaped a car

on mischief night and took off on your scooter,
mortified and with your next-door neighbor in pursuit.

At that age I got myself arrested in a high school parking lot
with a four pack of coolers in my lap. They cost me

one quick flash of my fledgling boobs, and then this officer
showed up and shined his department-issue flashlight on them

just a little longer than was necessary while he took the bottles
off me. I sat handcuffed to a desk chair while he filled out

his paperwork. None of this was badass, by the way, or
extraordinary, only desperate, a bid to let me play

two minutes in heaven in the closet with a script
that wouldn't have me working at a Taco Bell,

which is why I never figured out how to hit you back. Also
you never once came home from school to a ringing phone,

a bill collector asking where your mother's
mortgage payment was, late like it was every month

and you were also never late, you never frantically
counted out the minutes ticking while a little plastic bar sucked

up your pee. And Wells Fargo, you can go and fuck
yourself because you called all the time, and once

when I was in the bathroom peeing on the plastic stick. If
I'm being honest I'll admit I thought when I climbed in

your 1992 maroon Accord that I was some hot shit,
I thought finally I was going to blow this place like

a fucking princess, like, F you Catholic schoolgirls and F
your Benetton and your Depeche Mode and F your asymmetrical wedge

haircuts and I guess I did get somewhere but I did not ask
for this, this death descending between us like a fat feathered

disappointment in the middle of Belair Road between Saint
Michael's Church and a Taco Bell. So fuck this too.

Alcestis as Vigorous Cross Examination

PROSECUTOR: Are you prepared to answer?

WITNESS: A person can choose to act or be, but it's one or the other; the choice is definitional. Two ways of looking: from the inside or the out. Are you asking about my intentions, or about what happened?

PROSECUTOR: Will you answer for what happened?

WITNESS: Behind me were words, and in front of me are the things I don't know how to quantify. Let me explain.

PROSECUTOR: You would agree your choice has led to grief?

WITNESS: There were only so many things I could do with my hands and everyone needed all at once. Good intentions fumbled with the keys.

PROSECUTOR: What is your plea?

WITNESS: The positions I have taken : a bridge a prizefighter a mother a wife : and nothing tended.

PROSECUTOR: There is no version of this narrative that absolves you. Is that right?

ALCESTIS: A story doesn't speak when it's returned from dead. Every act is accidental until it's blooded with intention.

Alcestis as an Affidavit

1. I'm not here.

I am speaking from someplace else, meaning this is hearsay.

2. But sworn, therefore admissible. For certain purposes. At a trial.

3. Hearsay is an evidentiary problem with solutions.

One exception is for words while dying. Another is for someone "unavailable."

4. I don't know which one I am.

5. Do you want to know what I'm wearing now?

6. Do you want to know the trouble when it comes to proof? It can nearly always be disproven.

7. Narrative won't reduce to any single solid thing, the way a number will when you hold it to the light.

8. A number splits into its parts, retains its meaning. Words dissolve.

9. From the Latin, *dissolutus*, meaning "loose."

10. A woman might be loose or she might be held.

11. Fault lies in wait behind a door. Each cause latched in by a but-for.

12. I am getting ahead of myself. I want to explain.

13. How fault gives in to fault and assumes a line.

14. How the line explodes at points located with precision. With mathematics.

15. How points of destruction occur at the salpinx.

16. The word means "trumpet." Which rhymes with "strumpet."

17. But in my stories I am motherly. Domestic, sweet.

18. In Milton, for example, I appear to him washed clean. I, his wife I mean, who died giving him a child.

19. In the Franklin's Tale I am an honorable woman. I kept my vow.

20. As Hermione I am spared the necessary gloss. It's not my fault.

21. Only choices must be justified. Explained.

22. To Rilke I remained a bride, left no pain behind me, perfected.

23. And in Ted Hughes' Euripides, he wants us not to look too closely lest we be distracted by the obvious.

24. When we look, we see necessity. A problem solved, another in its place. All my voices say as much, in my name or someone else's. Interchangeable.

25. But virtue aligns with sacrifice in a way that it would not if I had stayed alive.

26. Our children suffer. The playwright engineers an ending that neatly satisfies.

27. It is better to be relieved of questions. Not to look too closely. Otherwise

28. we must consider whether I sought out Thanatos myself. Issued him an invitation, exited the house.

29. And we must assume that my marriage was a happy one. That Admetus was not prone to sudden violence. That there were no bruises, no red spatter, no kneeling down to scrub the bedroom wall all Sunday afternoon.

30. That the children never saw it. That I was clever.

31. Since I exchanged my suffering for theirs, they asked me for an explanation.

32. What can I tell them, except to explain?

33. That virtue is a point of view? In special cases, in the absence of agreement, vow or warranty.

34. That we don't always know disaster as disaster when it arrives. It wears disguises.

35. It watches and it waits beneath the willow tree.

Alcestis as a Gothic Disposition on an Autumn Afternoon

A good (woman) (home) abides
by certain principles.

The soffit is the underbelly.
(I am not fragile, I am only)
Segmented like a reptile,
the architecture keeps her low

and guarded when the storm
breaks (fractured, I will be fine)

In the morning I am both outside
the house and inside it.
I guide the children to the schoolbus
stop at the top of the road.

The house lolls all day in willow-shade
behind its portico-eyes,
its eaves. I calculate trajectories.

Assume that *x* is daylight,
that the doors will bang
and thrash, the wind will pick up.

Alcestis as Fibonacci Sequence

0.

you want to know the path by which a woman trades herself to death, well

it goes like this:

a kernel plants and then devours itself and leaves a trace

"a trace shows that someone has passed by but not who is"

Augustine's arithmetic of God in mortal creatures depends
upon a cause:

assuming a wind of constant velocity and objects of equal mass, the fallen leaves will
gather in the corners   around a building's quoins   the joints   which
in this case serve as obstacles to movement

in my case the first variable is that my mother broke a vow   before I was born
at least that is what I've always thought

that she left because she no longer sought to dedicate herself to God   but
I have asked myself recently if in fact she was no longer what He wanted and what
might have changed in the time that she was with him? it is possible that her own
immense secret was discovered

anyone would feel rage, disillusionment : to be cast out from the *de facto* family where the family *de jure* is inadequate

in any event there is the problem of the promise made and then regretted   even for reasons which could not have been foreseen

not even by the most reasonable, prudent person   (for me   math and laws are equivalent)

the firework carried onto the train platform initiates the first turning of the gear inside the Rube Goldberg machine   this promise explodes a need the body has not yet spoken

I call it a machine because it generates consistent motion

a cause or a way and a fundal pressure

whereby the preceding is made a cause of action, a pleading

resulting in : a birth

every violence a function of muscle, clenched and released

I.

Establishing shot through partially open vehicle window.
        Backseat of a long car. Fin-swooped whaler.
        Thigh-high harpoon-hoisted, petard and tusk.
        Head shake. Wait.
Not his car, nor the Thessalian Ocean
        I was expecting. Front seat,
        fin-swooped hardtop. I am younger, here,
        stringy-haired, gap-toothed,
rows of pale yellow stitches reticulating
        the bench seat and the mechanized leathery
        intuition: that attention paid is a piston
        driving memory. The older self is folded
into the glove, box, a negotiable instrument kited.
        Debit account dispenses forward travel
        and a jaunty tune. Come on down, next
        contestant. Behind Door Number One, boyfriend.
Behind the other, murkier, grandfather. Interchanged : interstate.
        When the game goes badly for me I'll assume it
        was my fault, not that the score is predetermined.
        Metal door creak and click and lock.
The seats are olive-colored. The dashboard,
        cool, texture of a lizard's skin. Lizards
        cannot warm themselves,
        they depend upon the sun, its constant
ministrations, to stay alive. A stasis maintained
        with reference to certain necessary outside forces.

Mathematics. Strange still life moving landscape
with girl, my history identifies
and circumscribes me. But everything sleeps,
so I do too, nose to tail, fishbowl eyes swiveling
from front to back. The facts — objective — change
depending on the camera lens. The view.
What right has any one of us to doubt
the destination a person gives herself if it means
she gets to go somewhere? Reflected light,
its sum and antecedents pinned
to the cold-foil recoil of recognition.

I.

Over-the-shoulder shot at grocery store check out. I have two books from the library in the rusty strip mall. Empty pizza shop at one end and a Rite Aid at the other. A Fotomat in the middle of the parking lot. We have driven the whole length of Hazelwood to get here even though the Enoch Pratt in Hamilton would be closer. My mother wants to cash a check and buy cigarettes and there is a grocery store across from this library. A Bi-Rite or a Rose's. It has a cork board near the check-out lines where people pin up their ads for babysitting or piano lessons or used cars. There are things they need and you can help them and that is good which is what we all should be. On this particular afternoon when we walk in there's a flyer with my mother's face. It says DO NOT CASH CHECKS but she'll try anyway. So I sit down on the faded bench. The gray metal on the crossbeams shows beneath the peeling wine-dark paint. I take out a book from my canvas bag. I also like this library better even though that isn't why we've come ~

you're a little young for that one a man says
nods toward *A Tree Grows in Brooklyn*
while he gently lays a bag of peaches on the top
of a brown paper shopping bag
that book he says again. Point of view
shift. Two weeks later we are back
because we have to return the books
we checked out and so we can buy tomatoes
for supper. I see the man, the thin strands of white
hair he combs over his red scalp. I say
it wasn't her fault, you know, and he wants
to know whose fault it was then. I pretend

I haven't heard the question because suddenly
I can see the cascade of fault in all of them.
Like tree bark petal-scabbing
over dying wood petals, only trying
to be alive, to do what it has been
inscribed to do. Stupid Katie marries
a man who drinks too much.
Johnny sick to death at Christmas.
Each mistake compounding and even
eating other mistakes and packing them
down and suffocating the tree until
the narrative is wormy white beneath.
And Francie will do it too,
won't she? I sit down on the sagging bench to wait again

2.

Some days count and some do not.
They grow one over another like

husks of tree bark. You can only peel them

down so far. I begin to number
them in a book. The cover swaddled in muted pink
and white cloth. I make a neat

chart at first, then a digit for each
day that passes : for good or bad.

These accumulate and come to stand
for "ideas" of how a day should be. A distance
is necessary. A depth of field.

Shallow focus shot, two figures foregrounded:

my mother, her feet buoyed upon the ugly
hassock, upholstered in a pixelated
print of brown and yellow pheasants,

reading the pink and white book.
Air rich with nicotine and tin

and points of view. I have some things to tell you,
she says,
and stubs her cigarette into a dish.

The white paper tube of it
crinkled at an angle
upon which the camera lingers.

Mother: Wait
Girl:

M: Where are you going
G: Upstairs

M: These things you've been writing
G: It's only math

M: Why are we both so angry
G:

3.

A pivot point: a fulcrum. A center
around which a fact achieves a stasis, or does not.

The beam splinters
the posts. The house comes down.

Ratio of the angle of the room to roof to two by four they marched and were therefore saved from the deluge when it came/and as for we who lived at the mouth of rivers

:: some overarching intellect imposed a sense of order upon the great catastrophe
:: so I was saved
:: beneath the water tongues began to knot themselves into sense
:: I reached into the gray-green for one
:: it swam willingly into my hands

5.

In the film *No Way to Treat a Lady*, Rod Steiger as Christopher Gill kills several elderly women who stand in for his recently deceased mother, a theater actress, a woman of many masks. Gill adopts flamboyant and even ridiculous disguises in order to earn his victims' trust. Once he has strangled them to death, he places a lipstick kiss on each of their foreheads. It is a strange film, made in the days before the twin ascendancies of forensic science and behavioral profiling, when audiences were satisfied with the absurdly and inexplicably villainous. "*Why not say what happened?*" and so on.

It was my mother's favorite. There was also *Gaslight*,
Wait Until Dark, movies characterized by the fetishization
of violence upon the female body; but I suspect,
without any evidence to confirm, that she loved
the film for its willingness to take
a mother to task. To subject
her to violence even if by proxy. And in her way
she was explaining how things were between us. Call it necessity, a kind
of imperfect self-defense. To act out what she felt against her own mother
would have been unthinkable.

8.

Low angle shot:

Two women come to visit.
While my mother looks
on, they carry off
the mewling child. A nurse
cries and I do not. Someone snaps
a photo. My legs,
my faded ditsy-printed
nightgown. The bed, the hand
resting on the not-
belly. Half a bouquet
wilting on the table visible
within the frame.

The eye tends to follow
the motion of the Fibonacci spiral
inward, towards its center, to seek the place
at which movement comes to rest. In nature,
the spiral tracks an outward path on which each new
point occurs farther and farther from the previous point. Like *pi*, *phi*
is restless. It continually moves toward what it is missing and cannot have:
fixture. Home. The weight of memory divided by the measure of time passed.

13.

The question becomes, then, not whose fault it was, but what fault is.
It becomes both those questions. The question is transformed
into questions. And in the meantime, the thing having
been done, grew. Or rather the waters rose. All rhetoric
functions in this way, accumulates a language around
the nub of injury, which is the question. After a while
a person learns to speak differently, but the muscle memory
remains. The atrophy a kind of vessel seeking its meniscus.

And the vessel wishes to be good but also needs. Its "argument
is built upon the shifting meanings

of such words as 'wrong' and 'wrongful,' and shares

their instability."

21.

No one
could accuse me of culpability, all traces
gone. We would never speak of it.

Some goddess made us a gift of snakes.

34.

Cut to:
Monologue, a woman stands naked on a theater stage, front light.

I would   like to break   everything.
There   does not seem   to be a   place
to put this   rage, so I   hold it to my breasts

and coo to it like a   baby. Slowly   the feeling
acquires   a face,
a fist. The mouth purses tight,

I place the   child into my   handbag,
close   it with a   satisfying
snap.   Lift the strap   to my shoulder.

My shoulder aches beneath this weight.

55.

Extreme long shot:

The race declared for me, my hand. Rocked back and forth within the cruising limousine : ceaseless layered frames of movement : Muybridge gallop : a ball thrown within a moving train : ball-body alive at constant speed : but to a person watching the chariot pass : ball-body catches light in glass and is not seen : the vehicle hastens to its glass destination : the woman inside : molt(en)(ing) : if I arc fast enough : to rip the engine from the track : and shatter : sharp wheel fragments churning up the grass : cindering the station : its window-eyes watching :

This happens and does not happen.

The train arrives and does not arrive. I climb from the car and stay inside it. Smooth down dress : iridescent : I billow to hot glass. Scale the church steps : scale the song arcing : glass door pivot. Cool stone & candle wax & arpeggio of breath wound tight. Each number on the scale corresponding to the sum of the preceding numbers until there is a transpositional error and we lurch into a chord. Arc in a wave. Like light. Admetus, my husband. We exit to the skene.

Alcestis as Saltine Crackers on the Tongue, Dissolving into a Paste, You Put Too Many of Them into Your Mouth at Once, You're Going to Choke

And then you do
When will you ever learn[1]
Your mother says[2]
Hand on her hip
Diaphanous scarf[3] of nicotine-tinged particulate and tar
Pulled tight around her throat[4]

1 Contributory negligence: the failure to take precautions for one's own safety. *See Potts v. Armour & Co.*, 39 A.2d 552, 555 (Md. 1944).

2 Looking as if she were alive. I call

3 Tareyton Cigarettes: There's *Something* About Them You'll Like!

4 Intervening, superseding cause: an event that occurs after a party's improper or dangerous action and before the damage that could otherwise have been caused by the dangerous act, thereby breaking the chain of causation between the original act and the harm to the injured person. *See Pittway Corp. v. Collins*, 973 A.2d 771, 789 (Md. 2009); *see also* Nighttime Ischemic, SWWIM EVERY DAY, 1.14.2019.

Whereas

To understand, you must be familiar with the play.
It's the version of the mythology that we know best.
There must have been a real woman like Alcestis. And she died.
She might have been a particulate solidified, in the throat, where speech resides.
Who knows how to interpret the story as its teller framed it? It's ambiguous.
Not easily sorted into one category or another.
The audience is uneasy with all this pomp. A dead wife resurrected.
A husband who's done a violent something not quite named.
A hunky strongman waiting in the wings to save her. A trace of farce. Even camp.
We read Heracles' lines in Harvey Fierstein's voice. We can't help it.
And then there are the questions raised and never answered.
Surely Admetus, the husband, has caused harm. But was it necessary?
And what about Alcestis? Her sacrifice is too pure.
We don't trust it. No woman is as innocent or austere as the writer makes her.
That she would leave her children so eagerly.
As if she'd planned her exit for some time. As if she desired it above all else.
Children play. Adults must act.
This is the rule by which drama wields its power.

Alcestis as a Kubrick Film Ending in a Line by Lynda Hull

The Killing *(film, 1956)*
Black Mare, *Lynda Hull (poem)*

Unglamorous, sallow, brown, but with the same ruined
flowers, windows peeled down like strips of paper,
headlights off. Eventually it wasn't cars in parking lots,
boys took me to the sullen rooms they rented
along trucking routes. The desk clerk might take
one look at me from above his reading
glasses and then shake his head. Mostly though
the clerks plucked room keys off their hooks and gave
us both an attaboy look, a go-get-em boyo, for the prize
I represented in my second-hand Gunne Sax, powder
blue, tulle skirt, the bodice crossed with sequins
like a pie lattice. Or it might have been the white satin
dress I wore to someone's high school harvest ball,
portrait collar, kitten heels, both lent to me by someone's
older sister who'd picked them up on sale at Sears. The boys
wore their fathers' good suit jackets, their bony shoulders
bolstered underneath the bunching fabric, or nubby
yellowed Oxford shirts and skinny ties just like Ric
Ocasek's when he drove girls home. Boys
with their caldera mouths, thick fingers, patches

of the fine dark hair that grew inside the smalls
of backs, in places where my fingers crept, boys
with eyes closed, boys looking to the side at water
glasses in their paper caps or at the printed roses
fading on the drywall's vine. Boys who waited silently,
impatiently, beside the door while I made searching
inquiry of sheets and carpet for the galaxy of sequins
fallen from the borrowed dresses. In such rooms
the television's always on and tuned
to something colorless. One night a boy slept beside
me while I watched Sterling Hayden cram
a pile of stolen cash into a suitcase, watched him labor
at it, sweat it, there was a flight he was supposed to catch
and a woman waiting for him and for that money.
It was too heavy to be carried on and so he had to check
it, and then the bag cracked open on the tarmac. Tenderly
the camera follows as the bills go soaring off, the idling
jet's engines propelling them at varying velocities, as stars
spin faster while they linger in the grip of gravity,
then meander orbits plotted for them by their own idle
involutions. Inevitably it seems we are undone by
mundane things, devoid of grandeur or significance:
an overloaded baggage cart, an X marked monthly,
faithfully, and then for nine months not, the sure thing
horse that breaks its leg in the final stretch. *What's*
the difference mumbles Sterling as the police approach him
and the screen falls dark. When the sleeping boy awoke
we stepped out into the humid nighttime air. He slipped

into the driver's seat while I stood there fumbling
with the lock he took his time with disengaging, not
looking at me even once. Years have passed since then
and I still search for schemas in what's been merely scattered,
and once I finally concede I watch reflected, in the window
glass, the stars dragging the weight of their own illuminations
into the rooms of this vast hotel, the past. What did we learn?

Alcestis as the Wire Hanger from Mommie Dearest

Mommie Dearest *(film, 1981)*

Int/Night—Faye Dunaway as Crawford entering her daughter Christine's idyllic bedroom, admiring the child who lies as if artfully composed for death, her arms neatly resting upon her satin sheets, her hair lying upon the pillow so as to convey the purity, the perfection, the angelic virtue of the girl. Crawford herself is both monstrous, in the exaggerated whiteness of the cold cream meant to preserve her youth, and splendid, even royal, in her cobalt-colored velveteen bathrobe.[1]

The hanger may assume these roles because of Crawford's internalized notions of femininity and particularly of female-oriented family loyalty. The wire hanger is to be distinguished from the pretty wooden and satin-dressed hangers Crawford has purchased for her adopted daughter. Wire is plain. It is unadorned, cheap, it makes nothing of itself other than what it is.[2]

And the hanger stands as well for the child's rebelliousness, which Crawford condemns as too masculine at various points in the film, or as too feminine, a status

1 Therein lies the crux, the problem of the film: Dunaway as Crawford as mania as mother makes of herself a penitential gash, a wound upon the sleeping child. The solitary wire hanger found in Christine's closet electrifies Crawford's fury and fuels the daughter's brutal punishment.

2 To call a man "wiry" is to identify his pluckiness, his "fight," his ability to stand back up when life has struck him a blow. A wiry man carries determination on his bones and little else. To call a woman wiry however is to euphemize her uselessness. A woman is to be composed, enrobed, curved. The wire hanger therefore stands for Crawford's fear that the drudgery of mothering will deprive her of her beauty.

Crawford equates with promiscuity. Neither state is acceptable in the mother's world as both are, in Crawford's mind, deviant. The child has been warned that she is to conform. Yet there is a wire in the child's blood and it carries electricity. The resulting shower of cleaning powder upon the blue-tiled floor, as Crawford succumbs to the apotheosis of her frenzy, may therefore be interpreted as a sexual act of mastery or an attempted chemical extinguishment, we can't be sure which.[3]

If a metaphor can do anything in literal fashion, it does so here, as the hanger bears the weight of the expectations hung upon it. There is the idea of social class, of Crawford's insecurity about her own upbringing among working people sparked by the vagueness of Christine's ancestry. Insofar as the child was orphaned during the Great Depression, Crawford must have assumed that Christine was born into a similar class and yet her presence in Crawford's home has come to represent a threat. Crawford seems to believe that the child will taint what she has achieved even as the child permits her to assume the privileged stature of motherhood.

Crawford plays *mater* with relish, dressing the child in expensive frocks, posing her for photographs, and preening with visible delight when her benevolence is remarked upon. Yet as Christine ascends to the luxurious heights of her mother's ambitions for her, Crawford's sadistic desires to discipline and control and even to destroy lurk beneath the shimmering surface and occasionally whip themselves into life.[4]

3 It is this ambiguity that fuels the scene. Crawford-as-mother, as sacrificial offering consumed by a fire of her own making, is enigmatic. The hanger is weaponized against the source of her anxiety and is also a cause of her anxiety, leaving Crawford at war with herself and with collateral damage done. The hanger holds — literally, wears — the fruits and evidences of Crawford's success as an object of male sexual desire and as a mother and its presence in her otherwise carefully curated home stands as a reminder that not everything can be controlled or anticipated.

4 These energies manifest as panic and rage directed at the site of domesticity, the home, the child's clothing, the child herself. The scene occurs in the one room of the home devoted exclusively to rest: the bedroom. Crawford's relationship with Christine is thereby irretrievably shattered.

The scene has become iconic for the way in which it memorializes the catastrophic end of the dream of a family for both parties involved. There can be no repose, no slackening, no moderation, according to this tableau; always the thing that vexes, that torments us, shelters within our costumes and, simultaneously, props them up. In the case of women, we hang ourselves upon our own desires to provide for our children, to ensure them a place in life, a good family, and in doing so we often maim them.

Alcestis as a Postulate and Some Instructions

1.

Some of these poems
are proofs

2.

Some of them
are *special cases*

3.

Taken together, as they must
be :   arithmetrical in

4.

-itiations.

5.

There is, first,
the postulate :

She *intended*

6.

And then the exception :

but did it do

any *good?*

7.

You can only

fix the value   for intention

8.

Rely

upon it

9.

until plans fail

10.

in which case

11.

12.

no matter

13.

Euclid's *a priori* thinking

14.

Once a postulate is proven there

is no squaring up at   its gate

15.

its trellised hysteria

16.

Along the path of definition
the child on one side
of the equation

17.

must equal
the woman on the other and

17.

she doesn't always
recognize

18.

when she is
passing through
the equal sign :

19.

it's so narrow there

Alcestis as the Dead Woman's Auto-Roman à Clef

Butterfield 8 *(novel, 1935; film, 1960)*
Starr Faithfull, 1906–1931

Here's Melpomene, two times over, replicated,
and here's the scene: a man, his wife, and me in her fur

coat. For warmth, for modesty, and for dignified
egress when I had nothing else to wear the morning

after. It's a riot. Now I'm dead. This little distance
brings the camera into focus. I thought he'd be

the roadway out and I climbed in. He popped
the clutch. And I fell out. Would you say it's funny,

my red Sunbeam Alpine roadster struck a roadblock, flew,
curvaceous hood streaking over sleek and gleaming tail,

and snuffed me out atop a mound of concrete rubble? Or
when the writer dropped me in the water lapping

at a steamboat's paddle, whichever means of manual
destruction of the muse that you prefer. Does it matter? Anyway,

it wasn't ecstasy or tragedy, you can't say that you don't like
the speed when your foot's on the accelerator, can you? Move

over, friend, some stories write the endings for themselves
and that's all that there is to them. Auto-written, autoerotic,

automotive, autocratic. You'll go on dressing me inside
that coat, naked underneath because as far as you can tell I'm Liz

Taylor. But I'm so much older. Older than the girl they based
the story on, older even than this kind of fiction, the lyric

wrinkling back upon itself: a secret message on an envelope.
Where drama equals one plus one, I'm twenty-nine or thirty.

Are you thinking what I'm speaking? I'm the figure fierce
inside the animal, the ripples on the greasy pelt standing

in for what's beneath, the woman who is still alive, the proof
of life. She has done so many things

that she should not have done and caused such pain
and oh, they were delicious while I did them.

Alcestis as Modern Love

I'll tell

you how it makes my knees quiver, makes me papery,
your inclination to fold me into something
categorical:

                    a swan. An airplane.

Engineered, less accidental.
Performative but

                    theoretical.
You, babe, would like to call your shot

with me, reliably. That's masculinity,
isn't it, I recognize it in you: your easy faith,
your sodium light. No washing out the sky

when all the eyes are on the diamond. You'd prefer
to deal in certainty, you're on and off, first or third
or not at all, a binary, but I'm a special case

                    so pick

a printing plate to start from. The pulp that makes
the paper. Isn't it just the filthiest thing?
The process makes an absinthe of the water.

But that isn't what you'd like to postulate. No,
it isn't right, the underlying cocktail
glowing in its certain pleasant way. Now we're talking

about me again. My woody crush, my mash. My—
shall we say it? Slurry. We are what we've absorbed—
and we deflect

what others see of us. Therefore

what we reflect is not what makes us. This is <axiomatic>
we say like light and now we've
been converted. What I'm getting at—

in my way, my deliberative foul-line arc—is how
I won't forget the uneven notes I've blown,
the guy I knew for two days, his hairy

back. The truth, which is the physics of it, and then,
the myth you want to make of it. Squared up,
swung hard, the perception

soaring

into the post-game
analysis we'll all remember,
true or not. Meaning plucked

from the little gesture, the signal, quite possibly
a fallacy. We assume intention from
the thing's momentum. We expect

that what they write about, good newspaper-
men, is new. That they grind it up, reality,

and go to print

                    with something significant.
The light's evaporating amalgam. The story.

Eave | Soffit | Gable | Willow

The (light) (house) (woman) desires breath
to burn.
(It) (she) will be an honest fire.

An opened bone becomes a window,
opens wide. A jagged
bone is planed like timber.
The wood is sanded into nooks
and afternoons; into bedtimes and *Goodnight,*
Moon.

The nooks are painted into pantries.
The pantries are stacked with apples, pumpkin
butter. Children playing hide and seek.

Chalk dust, garden hose. Birds in hand.
Front door creak.

Din of rain upon the roof.

Alcestis as Res Gestae[1]

Imagine the albumin becomes
the chicken's skin it doesn't
but it should
it is the perfect waterwhite
to make the flimsy rubber film
enveloping the yolky viscera and
otherwise the insides might blow out and go
soaring through the tattered shell to where
Admetus stands one morning after
exiting the shower he lifts
himself onto one foot gracefully how
like a bird he is and spins around
without stopping without speaking and
he looks at me the way a bird
is startled by an unexpected crash
ridiculous now to picture it again
these years later knowing I
am no less fragile and that it would
have been so much kinder not to bind him up
with all his shatter

1 "What kinds of things does history find out? I answer, *res gestae*: actions of human beings that have been done in the past. Although this answer raises all kinds of further questions, many of which are controversial, still, however they may be answered, the answers do not discredit the proposition that history is the science of *res gestae*, the attempt to answer questions about human actions done in the past." R.G. Collingwood, THE IDEA OF HISTORY.

Alcestis as Peripheral | Swift | Ominous Movement in the House

The eye's focus accumulates upon a central field,
a swiveling musculature. A kitchen table. Beneath the membrane,

a lens records. Text upon the skene observed: `[A toddler in his favorite overalls.]`
Text: `[A plate of seedless grapes and a sippy cup.]`

Workmen ring the willow tree, tuck
their ruddy hands into their pockets. Someone heaves an axe `[. . .]`

Text: `[The tree falls.]` The television
has been left to play its narrative, a field of players also like an eye

but looking back. From the landing atop the stairs,
Admetus thunders toward your instrument.

His shape is not inside your processor, not yet,
the eye has not been taught the precursive code, requiring

first the distillation of experience into digits. `[Zero, one.]` Assessment
as a kind of death or lingering internal reconfiguration.

Assessment as a prerequisite to pain, to sense,
which is prerequisite to leaving. When you regain consciousness

you will think about this more. The field will lie in darkness for an hour
or two. Alcestis is alive and dead, not here or there nor she nor I.

Eave | Soffit | Gable | Willow

On a Saturday morning

a light covering of snow lay
upon the pine tree in the front yard.

That night we were all very merry. The children
held paint chips to the walls.
I thought, we'll put a willow there,
out on the hill.
Very specific plans
were made.

(ambiguity) (expurgation)

A house will lie while it is open.

One window. One
door. That is enough

to admit
an interloper.

((about this (thing) (man) (fist) I am
ambiguous))

Once
we let a chipmunk in.
Fat striped thing. From one
end of the living room
to the other it

dashed and tumbled.
I put up a porch swing.
Sat outside rocking, in the evening.
Watched the bats wheel and spin and dive.

When the weather changes, late,
how do you tell?

Do you go inside and wait?

A better woman
would have felt
it in the joints. Would

have sought a remedy
for the smaller aches
before

Alcestis as Mentes Reae

O my bed, here I loosed my maidenhood beneath a man,
for whom I die—farewell! I do not hate you. You bring me to death
but I could not betray him.

Alkestis, *translated by Anne Carson*

Even the word, *incoming*,
like the arrival
of a bomb, the bright-fused,
incendiary blessing, everything
made clean and wicked
as
we were blossoms,
we pulse-lapsed : received : were
bruised, seeded, *appels d'offres*
sauvage. Roughed up in our
calloused willow-work. Day
by fetid day the house buzzed
with flies and I

        considered what I'd done

made preparations for my leaving

        and nothing and everything happened

at once

the children slept in their neat flannels

the arc of my work

the arc of the house above us sloping

Panopticon

In the morning
I sit inside, windows slumped
into plaster.

A mind sees only outwards or
refuses to be seen.

Memory taps the nail of experience
into place. Winds

a path of string from one nail to the
next.

This is a dark house.

In the afternoon
I sit outside. Birds wheel
and dive.

The house has such a mind. It turns
heavily upon itself with the sound of
satin on carpet. With an intensity of
gravity.

There are interiors which must be

drawn around the shoulders for

warmth.

In the evening I sit outside
alone. Bats wheel and dive
until the moon drops
its bright curtain.

(He will like me if I stay)

(He will destroy everything if I
leave)

(I don't know how to leave)

Alcestis as the Elegant Proof

Hours after, the woman's resurrection is a favor,
an arrangement. An exchange agreed, for value,
where "value" we assume is synonymous

with good. Assumption no. 2 in this equation
is that one life is worth as much as, no more than,
any other. This theorem could not prove itself,

so she set out for Hades with her calculator. Imagine
you are Thanatos, waiting patiently at the door,
maybe tapping your foot a little and out walks a wife,

and not the man that you expected. A trade presumes
the constancy of *x*. No matter how the variable changes
hands, moves along love's bucket-brigade, the *x* remains

itself: tomato juice. Suitcase. Cardigan sweater. Thanatos
has other doors to knock on so why not take her
if she arrives pre-wrapped for the grave and makes no fuss

about the muddy grass around the stone. I chose Alcestis
because she seemed to be the best form, *x* considered,
for what needed to be done but I didn't see at first the duplicity

of the role I'd chosen. Like my children, who sat cross-
legged all in a row, watching SpongeBob. They suspected
nothing, while in another room I solved for virtue

and arrived at zero. O Heracles. What luck was his last-
minute entry on the scene, and with what skill he found
the answer to my problem. I felt a swell of gratitude that was,

at first, immeasurable. A crowd of people gathered, asked me
questions. Why, they said, and what was it like, down there,
and were you punished for what you did? I could not speak.

Alcestis as the Doomed Mignonette*'s Cabin Boy, Parker*

To preserve one's life is generally speaking a duty, but it may be the plainest and the highest duty to sacrifice it. —R v. Dudley and Stephens (1884)

went down
for tea
it was a little
weather

easy
and suddenly sea
water everywhere

and dark
no air
someone hauled
me upwards
heavy wet
we rocked
and waited in the dinghy

the ship sank
fast
a seaman dragged in

a turtle
we ate it
with a tin
of turnips

naught
to drink
but all the sea
and I was tired

under the harsh
sun
and Dudley got a funny
look

frightened
"What, me?"
I said when he sank his
knife
into my neck

and I let my hand fall
into the cool water
The light returned
an infinity of fingers
to me from beneath
the blue nebulae

and I think
I must have been
very sweet
to them

On the Stairs: An Auto-Critique

Like lovers silhouetted
through a turret window

we might as well be Greek for thinking
our tower could be free from sorrow

now, look:

my sleeves are scented with calamity
and violets

against that heft you lost
resolve

and I will not ascend the stair again
having laid my foot

where it should not have been

I wonder what the neighbors
thought, that afternoon

the front door swung open
wide

exposing you   inside
and crouched
upon the staircase   hands

around your needs
too large a man
to sit this way

and in the end it mattered not
at all that I blotted

up the spattered paint
before it ruined everything   the policeman gently
lifted your wrist as if in   invitation

Alcestis as the String of Numbers in a Man's Mouth at 3 a.m.

It was the one
thing they both wanted, to
own a house and live out their days there, then three
days after they unpacked he asked her for
something to help him sleep. He took five
of her pink Benadryls. He slept six

hours restlessly that night and six
the next and then he stopped sleeping. Once
when his psychosis was at its worst five
months later and the two
of them were climbing into bed she cried for
ten minutes while he stared at her not blinking. She'd called 911 three

times by then and three
times the ER sent him home after six
hours' observation. That was when she gave up waiting for
a solution, a reckoning, an explanation, and wondered
if this was it, the rest of her life, this. All she wanted now was to
climb into the bathtub in the morning, five

or ten minutes of floating in the still water, another five
in the shower so her hair at least was clean, then she outfitted the three

children with their backpacks and lunch totes and drove them to
school. After that she gave the office six
distracted hours, which was all she could afford, and one
exhausted hour in the evening after she put the kids to bed. For

months that's how it was, and he used up his four
months of disability, and the mortgage payment was almost five
grand, and they owed the contractor for carpet installation on the first
floor, and the countertops guy, and the arborist who dug out three
trees that were half-dead when they moved in, and sixteen
hundred for the landscaping that wasn't even finished yet. At two

in the morning she wasn't sleeping either anymore, and she turned to
him one night and looked at him, hard, examining his face for
any sign he understood what he was doing to them both, his six-
month separation from reality had them in the hole by five
thousand dollars so far, and three
times she asked him, do you even remember me? I only want

to know that you'll come back, and he, as he had begun doing, pulled at one
ear and cleared his throat and rocked back and forth and counted off two six nine
eight three five five five five five five five five.

Whereas

Did you think that we would spell it out for you?

Explain the puzzle? Make it all fit?

There's no life in that.

Off the stage no one tells you where to stand or what to say or hear or do.

Sometimes you have to read between the lines, to coin a phrase.

Find your own mark and hit it. Keep your elbows in.

Watch out for the *machina* when she descends.

Alcestis as a Failed Suicide

The area
postrema

located
in the brain stem

operates via
a geometry

in which the route
to departure

is determined by
the rate

at which a bolus
(in this case,

sweet little oblong
peaches)

passes
through the pharynx

multiplied by
the inverse

of the
gag reflex

and divided
by

the time between
one phone call and another

Alcestis as X in a Well-Ordered System

My mother and me and *Madame X*.
Such shoulders she had. But which woman
do I mean? you ask. I don't know.

I am looking at the three of us,
smeared in vague into this neat square.
Tilted at a crazy angle. Who took

this photo? I have no idea. Ideas are fleeting,
they fleet. They are not susceptible
of portraiture, but we do try. This was the year—

I was twelve maybe, or thirteen—of being
inconsolable and she finally asked me, what?
what do you want? And the truth

was unspeakable so I said art. She drove us
one weekend to an exhibition. We walked
and looked and admired and someone took

this photo in my hand and there I am, receded
into all that hazy cocoa and velvet, the camera flash
reflected in my lenses. You see what I've done.

A painting in a photo in a poem. There is
the most lovely satin ribbon running
through it but it will be sullied if you hold it

so don't. Please. I telephoned her—my mother,
not the X/x of the portrait or this poem—what,
thirty years after we stood there awkwardly

grinning. Called her *mommy*. Could she
please. I said. Please. Could she come and get
me and she could not. So I went home

in the pale blue gown they'd draped me in
when I arrived the week before, mouth blacked
through the efforts of the ambulance

man. The strings wouldn't tie in the back. Not all
the way, which is how these things go,
always teased, never polished off. The loosened

gown slipped down one shoulder, the skin
beneath exposed white, creamy, milky, scandalous.
A taxi took me back to my apartment.

You see, I warned you: I said let the ribbon go,
there is no need to for you to catch it. It dirties
when you finger it, the skin's own oils insinuate

themselves onto the sanctity of the fabric's glossy
surface. This field I stand in now has the same
ochre, same lumpy furrow, and it recedes into whatever

it is that holds it still. There is a ribbon in it.

Eave | Soffit | Gable | Willow

The weather has been
as expected. In the afternoon

the sky glowers
low. I cannot stand beneath

it without folding. The grass
opens to receive me.

A woman
lies down upon a table.
(this is the church, this is the steeple)

To make a home, she must
deduce:
that there is no light without
consumption. No
consumption without fuel.

She feeds herself to the bricks
and nails and lumber

and they lie down on her.
She ignites

(all the people)

Alcestis as Beads on an Abacus String

Alive. No, dead. . . . Oh, read it either way.
Alcestis, *translated by Gilbert Murray*

What is still me is also what waits—expects—
to be away. An arithmetic of loss. Sub-
traction. Moved to one side. Not counted. Smooth wooden
bead of glitch (code) in which accuracy means "at
the bone." The idea dependent upon what lies
and what speaks or counts. Scaffold on which is hung a rag(e) and paper
song. Not one inch real of me until reduced
numerically, this abatement in mass and ownership an infinity as wide
and high-strung as breath. As one cell respires
into another : until all of them, numerators, make : a lung. As
an intake collides with exhalation and desires
what cannot be kept, transforms what cannot be defined except
by what is lost. Stripped bare. Made nude upon the hill-
side. Ossified until the shatter. I take my place upon the wire.

Alcestis as a Throat Become a Well

Who
speaks
for me
when I cannot
will I be gently
soothed until
the chilly hands
drop their
fluttering
at the breast
the head
once more
conjoined to body
and air
restored
to lung
and who
will dispel
what   choked
me to   wherever such
things go   the stony
vault
for all ejected
reliquiae

they
ask me what
has happened
and I cannot say
that between my
brain and belly
now there is
a well   sunk
by the man
I followed
to the
riverbed
who made me kneel
before
his slick
and stony
vault
until my throat
was sore and
my hands were
limp   from
grappling   and
my husband
cannot
fathom my
stillness
now or
my refusal

to explain
that the woman
split
in half and fused
again   is satisfied
with what her brain
and belly say
to one another
that the well   its passage
cleared
swallows all its water

Alcestis as a Crane, a Lady, and the Rafters

For S.V.

Admit it, lover: you think of me when days
lie down and drop their heat.

Far enough away from you, I swoon
into a leafy season,

return to our proscenium. Demi-man,
blue-pigeon-breast, I played you out

like you played me. It's just the script
I got, every line a little more

acute. The *deus ex machina,* descended
from the rafters. I was to climb on and ride

and fly away. Applause, applause. Then exit
forestage and fall. I'd been so very

eager to make my getaway.
In my haste, I chose (sigh)

the wrong play. That's the diva's plight.
It's Medea who goes free; Alcestis dies.

What a choice to force on anyone?
There's good or there's pragmatic, a terrible dilemma;

synonymous alternatives, subjectively,
depending on the objective (wink) Either way,

nothing will be the same for me. You took
your cue before the lights went down. Still,

thank you for the flight, my gray
bird. My Thanatos for one glorious

dying season. My synecdoche
of autumn sedum, charcoal and necessity.

Eave | Soffit | Gable | Willow

The house breathes   rattles
coughs beneath
the storm.

The children look
to me for a signal. I look
at myself

and orient

(expurge)

Willow on the hill arcs toward
dim

shakes   loose

(lizard eye)
blinks
the children to their
beds

(sleep)

if she does not
get back up if she turns
onto her stomach

if the (woman) runs
and takes the children with her (safe)

but (I) am not (her) I did not
take them

Whereas

Were you expecting Areopagus?

That is, also, the wrong play. We won't tell you whom to blame.

You've seen the cast of characters. You know them as well as anyone.

Assuming the script is truthful. Who knows?

Which one's the hero and which is the villain?

And no blaming Death. He does what he does, even when he's been invited.

One of them's a coward. One too courageous for their own good.

The children at least are innocent. And they will grow older, take their own stages.

Should we forgive them now for what they'll do?

Should we wait and see?

This is the original problem play. Have you solved it yet?

It's not so easy once the math gives way.

Solution

You ask why I married him, then. Everyone
asks this, and what can I say? except that he
was what I was enumerated for at that time

and place, where time and place equaled
what a girl could know because it's what she'd
lived so far. Every inch of me was sanded

down to match an answering pectoral,
a bicep. I tuck myself in.
There was the moment, I was twenty,

I lay atop his belly watching
breaths exchange within the mystery
of his person, in and out, the pulse gently

domestic, not at all erotic, and I appraised
his face, its planes and angles. I wondered,

could I love him? Because if I could not,
I should go home.

Points and Authorities

Alcestis as . . .

. . . Res Ipsa

Res ipsa loquitur means "the thing speaks for itself." Cicero coined the phrase in 52 BC, delivering an argument on behalf of a man charged with murder. Everyone knew the man had committed the crime. Cicero did his best but advocacy has its limits; the man was convicted and sent into exile. On that sort of record the term might have gone out of use, at least legally speaking, but it came roaring back in 1863.

In that year, the English Exchequer Court decided the case of *Byrne v. Boadle*, 159 E.R. 299. A man, Byrne, was walking along a road in Liverpool when a barrel of flour fell from the window of a shop and crashed onto his head. Byrne sued the shop owner. He couldn't testify because he had no memory of the event but another man, Critchley, had seen it. The problem was Critchley couldn't say how or why the barrel had fallen from the window. Without direct evidence of fault, the court could have ruled against poor Byrne but he won anyway. He argued that barrels do not ordinarily fall out of windows when people are being careful, and the shop owner was the only person with barrels of flour. Advocates today fall back upon *res ipsa loquitur* when it is difficult to say exactly what went wrong. Some narratives speak for themselves.

. . . Fibonacci Sequence

"[T]he trace of the Trinity appears in creatures.": *See* Augustine, *De Trinitate*.

Thomas Aquinas responded in his *Summa Theologiae*: "I answer that, every effect in some degree represents its cause, but diversely. For some effects represent only the causality of the cause, but not its form; as smoke represents fire. Such a representation is called a 'trace': for a trace shows that someone has passed by but not who it is. Other effects represent the cause as regards the similitude of its form, as fire generated represents fire generating; and a statue of Mercury represents Mercury; and this is called the representation of 'image.'"

"[T]he firework carried onto the train platform": In 1924 Helen Palsgraf stood upon the platform at the Long Island Railroad station with her children. Two men hurried ahead of her as the train pulled in. One of them dropped a package and it exploded. It was a box of firecrackers. The explosion knocked over a scale and the scale fell onto Mrs. Palsgraf. (So much of the law derives from errant barrels and bomb-tumbled scales.) Benjamin Cardozo wrote the opinion, one of the most famous American tort cases, still taught to first year law students everywhere. In *Palsgraf v. Long Island R.R. Co.*, 162 N.E. 99 (N.Y. 1928), he announced a theory of proximate cause that remains the standard. A defendant is not responsible for an injury unless the injury was objectively foreseeable. It must be possible to trace a cause from its beginning to its end or the cause dissolves into smoke.

"Why not say what happened?": *See* Robert Lowell, *Epilogue*. When Alcestis returns from the dead, she is silent. Perhaps it is better to hold one's tongue than mouth someone else's words. The knife in the preceding sentence has two edges and no handle.

Its "argument / is built upon the shifting meanings // of such words as 'wrong' and 'wrongful,' and shares // their instability.": *Palsgraf* again.

"Some goddess made us a gift of snakes": Alcestis married Admetus. Apollo also loved Admetus. Admetus gave all the props to Apollo, causing a barrel to fall or a package to blow up, and Apollo's twin, Artemis, complained of injury. As a direct and proximate result of her jealous rage she filled the couple's honeymoon suite with snakes. This was one red flag or risk attendant upon the marriage and Alcestis readily assumed the risk like a burden or a glory.

. . . Saltine Crackers on the Tongue, Dissolving into a Paste, You Put Too Many of Them into Your Mouth at Once, You're Going to Choke

"Looking as if she were alive. I call": *See* Robert Browning, *My Last Duchess*. Enough said about this.

. . . the Dead Woman's Auto-Roman à Clef

On June 8, 1931, twenty-five-year-old Starr Faithfull's body washed up on a Long Island beach. There are reasons to believe her death was not accidental or the result of suicide. She was badly bruised for one thing, and she had taken or been given Veronal, a strong sedative, before she died. The levels of the drug in her system would have rendered her unconscious or immobile, making it unlikely she walked into the water on her own. She had a lot of sand in her lungs, suggesting she drowned close to the shoreline. And there was a likely suspect. Andrew J. Peters, a wealthy and well-connected politician, had been sexually abusing Faithfull since she was a child of eleven. A man like Peters might have found it necessary to silence someone like Faithfull, and many believed at the time that he had.

Before her death, Peters paid Faithfull's family $20,000, funds earmarked for the young woman's medical care and therapy, but he made more payments afterward, suggesting he was being extorted. The family wrote to him to ask for more money shortly before Faithfull's body was found, and for this reason some suspected the family of being involved in Faithfull's death. It is possible that local gangsters had also begun extorting Peters with information about the abuse. This was 1931 after all, the Golden Age of organized crime.

But Faithfull was a severely traumatized woman, and she had written and spoken of suicidal urges before her death. Investigators were confident she ended her own life. Her family was convinced she had been murdered. Her death garnered significant media attention at the time and has continued to fascinate writers, especially writers of so-called true crime. One such writer was Jonathan Goodman, author of books like *The Killing of Julia Wallace*, *Bloody Versicles*, and *The Christmas Murders*. Goodman theorized in his book, *The Passing of Starr Faithfull*, that she had been kidnapped by mobsters and questioned in hopes of obtaining more blackmail material. Two other men, reporters for *The New Yorker*, thought she had been murdered for teasing a man with the promise of sex on the beach. The implication was that any man would have done the same, that a harlot got what she deserved.

Faithfull's diary found its way to the novelist John O'Hara, who relied on it to write *BUtterfield 8*, published in 1935. The diary itself has since disappeared but we have the mythology that was made of it. According to an article in *The Baltimore Sun*, the notebook may have been turned over to Peters in the same way Sylvia Plath's journals were turned over to Ted Hughes. Faithfull's diary was never published; arguably neither were Plath's.

O'Hara's novel transforms Faithfull into the character of Gloria Wandrous. The two women share backstories and sullied reputations. In the book, Wandrous neatly dies when she falls from the deck of a boat and is caught in its paddlewheel. This is a gruesome if apt metaphor for the tendency of respectable society to systematize the destruction of those who refuse to be respectable. The novel was made into a film starring Elizabeth Taylor in 1960. Wandrous' sex work in the book was toned down for movie audiences whose sensibilities would be offended by the principles of free market economics applied to sex. On the other hand, her death was sexed up and given a thrilling new treatment. This Wandrous, desperate to reform and extricate herself from an adulterous affair, speeds along scenic highways in a bright red sports car pursued by her married lover, played by Laurence Harvey. She escapes his lust only by spectacularly crashing. The crash is the culmination of a scene that plays out over four minutes of silence except for purring engines. Taylor's car careens through the air as she squirms and shrieks within and then comes to rest upon the ground, crushed, its mechanized ecstasy exhausted: another metaphor, this one campier and more voluptuous than O'Hara's. Harvey's character goes home to his wife who welcomes his return. He, not Wandrous, is the final girl in this story.

. . . Res Gestae

Translated from the Latin, res gestae means "things done" or "things transacted."

Nascent law follows one of two possible routes, statutory and common. Common law is case law, decisions announced by appellate courts based on their critiques of completed trials. Trials proceed by evidence. Evidence is either admitted, meaning that it can be considered by a jury, or it is not. Judges decide whether evidence can be admitted; in doing so, they exercise discretion. Discretion is judgment, so the resulting formulation or equation is circular: judges make law by judging.

In general, judges do not admit evidence that is hearsay. "Hearsay" is another term of art, something like what people mean when they condemn rumor as untrustworthy, but the legal version is much more specific: a trap for the unwary advocate. At one time, "res gestae" meant statements that ordinarily would be treated as hearsay, but were spoken in a way so closely connected with a crime that they could be considered part of the event itself. *See, e.g.*, *Wilson v. State*, 181 Md. 1, 3–4 (1942) (holding that "[e]vidence of declarations and acts, which are an immediate accompaniment of the act charged and so closely connected with the main fact as to constitute a part of it, and without which the main fact might not be properly understood, are admissible as a part of the res gestae.") In other words, the law presumed that statements could be bound up with acts, could be acts themselves, and where this was true the statements could be admitted into evidence just like a gun or a crime scene photograph.

. . . Mentes Reae

Literally, "guilty minds."

To successfully prosecute a crime, a prosecutor must prove the *actus reus*, or the physical elements of the charge: the things the law says must be done to accomplish the thing the law says must not be done. Most serious crimes also require proof of intent (or "mind"). There are different kinds of *mentes reae*. A person might have acted purposely, meaning the person intended to do the thing he did; recklessly, meaning the person must have known harm was very likely to occur; or negligently, meaning that the person was merely hapless. A crime committed with intent is far more serious than an accident.

Intent is rarely proved directly. People usually do not announce that they intend to commit crimes (though sometimes they do, sometimes with the force of law, in which case the person may be a President or one of the President's toadies). Intent is usually proved circumstantially, by inference. Jurors are asked to look into the house, say, or between the lines of things that have been said, and apply what they know of human behavior to the circumstances they see there. In the house. Or in the spaces between words spoken, which is its own kind of evidence.

. . . the Doomed *Mignonette*'s Cabin Boy, Parker

In 1884, a lawyer named Want hired one Dudley to transport a yacht, the *Mignonette*, from England to Australia. Dudley hired a crew to assist him: Stephens, Brooks, and a cabin boy, Parker. They departed from Southampton in May.

In early July the ship sank in stormy weather off the coast of Africa. The three men and Dudley climbed into the ship's dinghy with such provisions as they could quickly salvage, but they lost their stores of water and had nothing with which to fish. Thereafter they languished and starved beneath the star-dogged Moon.

According to Dudley later on, when he was on trial for Parker's murder, it was customary for sailors in such circumstances to draw straws. The man drawing the short straw would be sacrificed—killed—to save the others. If this was true, the men took no chances with their own lives. Parker had drunk seawater which made him ill and likely to die (according to Dudley; Parker, of course, was dead and unavailable to testify). Dudley convinced Stephens that the boy should be the one to save the rest, the lack of Parker's informed consent notwithstanding, and he took out his knife with Stephens looking on. Brooks took no part then, although he did once the deed was done. Eventually, the men were rescued by a German ship, the *Montezuma*. They were transported to England and taken into custody. After a trial they were sentenced to death. The sentences were quickly commuted.

In one account, Parker is said to have murmured, "What me?" as Dudley loomed over him, his knife glinting in the sunlight.

The case of *R. v. Dudley and Stephens* is one of several that consider the permissibility of harm to one in order to benefit another. The general public was fascinated with the stories of shipwrecked men, sometimes women and children, stranded on the open ocean with no or dwindling resources. Géricault's *Raft of the Medusa* was shown in 1819, confronting exhibitiongoers with persuasive evidence of suffering off the West African coast. In 1820, the American whaler *Essex* sank in the Pacific. Many of the surviving sailors remained alive by cannibalizing the remains of their colleagues. Melville transformed the story of the *Essex* into *Moby-Dick*. Of course it is far more comfortable to debate choices when one does not have to make them.

The fates of sailors charged with these kinds of crimes varied. The public sympathized, believing the men did only what was necessary to survive. Courts understood this. It was common at this time to impose the death penalty with a recommendation for mercy, so that often the sentences were not carried out. But it was one thing for sailors to break the second oldest taboo, and quite another to break the first. Lord Coleridge—great-nephew of Samuel Taylor Coleridge, and therefore no stranger to shipwrecked crews—wrote the decision of the court in Dudley's case:

> To preserve one's life is generally speaking a duty, but it may be the plainest and the highest duty to sacrifice it. . . . The duty, in case of shipwreck, of a captain to his crew, of the crew to the passengers, of soldiers to women and children, as in the noble case of the *Birkenhead*; these duties impose on men the moral necessity, not of the preservation, but of the sacrifice of their lives for others, from which in no country, least of all, it is to be hoped, in England, will men ever shrink, as indeed, they have not shrunk.

Necessity sometimes requires sacrifice and sometimes forbids it. Necessity, it is argued, sometimes requires the sacrifice of another whether the other knows it or not.

Rosie and Gracie Attard were born conjoined at the abdomen in 2000. Their parents, Rina and Michelangelo Attard, refused to abort the pregnancy. They also refused surgery to separate the twins, even though one of the girls, Rosie, had severe brain damage and was slowly killing her sister. Gracie was expected to survive the surgery. Rosie was expected to die. If they were not separated, they would both die within six months. The matter made its way to the courts.

Lord Justice Ward of the Court of Appeal of England and Wales decided that proceeding with the surgery in order to save Gracie's life was legally permissible. *See Re A (Conjoined Twins)*, 2 WLR 480. He discussed the medicine involved, the views of the girls' medical team, and the preferences of their parents. He discussed the legal principle of necessity, referencing *Dudley and Stephens*. He distinguished legality from morality, a difference the public often forgets but lawyers never do. The surgery went forward. Rosie died on November 7, 2000. She is buried on the island of Gozo in Malta.

Parker's remains were buried at sea.

. . . a Throat Become a Well

An advocate begins, yes, by defining terms, in which case, the terms of art are "throat" and "well."

A throat is a vessel or a conduit, typically narrower than what it joins, meaning that a throat is vulnerable and tender, the point at which a siege might best be directed.

A well is deep. It must be fathomed; it might be drawn from or on. A weary traveler drinks from a well. A woman waits by one. When she drinks she is alive. She rushes to speak of her experience, or so the Gospel tells us. *See* John 4:7–31.

One of the consolations of advocacy is that an advocate, for the most part, speaks for another and not for herself. This can be liberating, especially for one who hesitates to speak for herself for her own reasons. Perhaps the speaker has returned to life from death. Perhaps the speaker has *seen some things*. Seeing sometimes is a grief. To advocate for another is to assume a role, one that can be defined, refined, rewritten, revised. And in time made into poetry.

To advocate for the self is more complicated. Seeing sometimes is a grief.

Euripedes' *Alcestis* is an extraordinarily strange play. It premiered in the fourth daily slot at the City Dionysia Festival in Athens in 438 B.C. This was the slot reserved for satyr plays, which were not only comedic but coarse. Satyrs chased nymphs and drank a lot of wine. They belched and farted. Think: *Bridesmaids*, or *Knocked Up*, or National Lampoon's anything. Audiences were flummoxed, and not only because the play mixed comedy with tragedy. (We so much want to put things into binary categories. Euripedes said fuck that, which is one way of saying that *Alcestis* is a "problem play.")

The story also featured a woman heroically making a difficult moral choice. Women were not supposed to do that in Greek society. They were virgins in their fathers' homes or wives in their husbands' homes. A respectable woman was not supposed to be seen in public. Women could be priestesses or witches, but they wielded no main character energy in those roles. More than anything, a woman who was a mother was expected to remain with her children. The Greeks didn't know what to do with Alcestis, this wife and mother who so readily ceded her place so that her husband might remain alive. They were uncomfortable with the inferences that arose around a man who permitted her to go, who might even have been responsible for her leaving. They could not begin to fathom that their civilization built the house in which these characters read the lines given them.

Into that weird house strides Heracles, the great savior. He gets drunk, fulfilling at least that expectation for theatergoers, but his buzz is harshed by news of Alcestis' death. He does the only thing he can, which is to hike up his trousers and walk down into hell. He brings the dead woman back, still wrapped in her shroud. Admetus doesn't recognize her at first. Something significant about her has changed. She does not explain. The play ends. The people in the bleachers gather up their things and go home.

An advocate explains but there might be limits to what the advocate can confidently say because the advocate must speak for another. An advocate is like a narrator with a limited point of view. Only so much can be known under circumstances like these.

How much easier it would be if Alcestis would speak for herself but her route to speech is blocked by what she has seen.

The throat is the route to speech, the road between the well in the woman's belly and the tongue. When the block is cleared the well below spouts water. The water is collected, cooled and sanctified. We call this a story. There are many stories. When the stories overflow their vessels and mingle, achieve a common sense of direction, a current, when they sculpt beds that glisten underneath the water, when the river's very opaqueness becomes its name, its claim to sanctuary:

we call this myth.

Acknowledgments

I wish to thank the editors of the following journals where these poems first appeared:

Birmingham Poetry Review: "Alcestis as a Trial, an Ekstasis, a Whereas, or a Problem," "Alcestis as a Hon, but Not the Kitschy, Cute Kind," "Alcestis as an Affidavit," "Alcestis as a Kubrick Film Ending in a Line by Lynda Hull"

Rabbit [a journal of nonfiction poetry]: "Alcestis as Fibonacci Sequence"

Denver Quarterly: "Alcestis as the Wire Hanger from *Mommie Dearest*," "Alcestis as a Failed Suicide," "Alcestis as the Doomed *Mignonette*'s Cabin Boy, Parker"

The Ending Hasn't Happened Yet (anthology): "Alcestis as X in a Well-Ordered System"

EPOCH: "Alcestis as a Postulate and Some Instructions"

A Velvet Giant: "Alcestis as Mentes Reae"

I also wish to thank Stephen, as always; Han and Amorak, for believing in this "problem play" book and in its playwright; Cathryn Hankla, Thorpe Moeckel, Karen Bender, Patricia Spears Jones, Liz Poliner, Eve Ettinger, Jonathan Pyner, Kelly Sawin, Matthew Lee, Michelle Acker, and Tyler Starks, who saw versions of these poems well before they were ready for primetime; Wayne Sutherland and Colette Fugere, for years of support and kindness; Lynn Melnick; Amanda Newell, for being a necessary badass; Charles Gilman and Briggs Bedigian, for their support and kindness and, in particular, for stoically disregarding my vestiary eccentricities; Amy and Emily, for the letters to my soul and the way my voice breaks when I get to "each life has its place"; and Mrs. Wendy Parker, for seeing a poet in me when everybody else saw a miscreant. And for all the miscreants.

JENNIFER A SUTHERLAND is a poet, essayist, and attorney in Baltimore. She is the author of *Bullet Points* (River River Books, 2023) and *House of Myth and Necessity* (River River Books, 2026). Her work has appeared in *Birmingham Poetry Review*, *Hopkins Review*, *Best New Poets*, *Denver Quarterly*, *Cagibi*, *EPOCH*, and elsewhere.

RIVER RIVER BOOKS was founded by Amorak Huey and Han VanderHart in March 2022. Inspired by the idea that you cannot step in the same river twice, two poetry editors join together to publish (at least) two exceptional poetry titles a year, as well as the Plainwater Nonfiction Series.

Poetry Catalog

An Eye in Each Square, Lauren Camp, 2023
Bullet Points: A Lyric, Jennifer A Sutherland, 2023
Dear Memphis, Rachel Edelman, 2024
A Geography That Does Not Hurt Us, Carla Sofia Ferreira, 2024
Pastoral, 1994, Joe Wilkins 2025
Your Mother's Bear Gun, Corrie Williamson, 2025
Field Notes, E.G. Cunningham, 2025
Encounters for the Living and the Dead, Jameela F. Dallis, 2025
Antibody, Elane Kim, 2026
House of Myth and Necessity, Jennifer A Sutherland, 2026
Scythe, Elizabeth Sylvia, 2026
Fifty Mothers, Preeti Vangani, 2026
The Visible Field, Zoë Ryder White, 2026
Snails of the Apocalypse, Martha Zweig, 2026
Turn a Girl to Salt, Janet McAdams, 2027
Little Automata of the Deciduous Forest, Mirande Bissell, 2027
Whale Garden, Carolyn Oliver, 2027

Plainwater Nonfiction Series

There Is News Along the Ohio River, Beth Gilstrap, 2026
Backyard Alchemy, J.D. Ho, 2026